Blue Banner Biography

Mary J. Blige

Jennifer Torres

Mitchell Lane
PUBLISHERS

P.O. Box 196
Hockessin, Delaware 19707
Visit us on the web: www.mitchelllane.com
Comments? email us: mitchelllane@mitchelllane.com

Mitchell Lane PUBLISHERS

Copyright © 2008 by Mitchell Lane Publishers. All rights reserved. No part of this book may be reproduced without written permission from the publisher. Printed and bound in the United States of America.

Printing   1   2   3   4   5   6   7   8   9

Blue Banner Biographies

Akon	Alan Jackson	Alicia Keys
Allen Iverson	Ashanti	Ashlee Simpson
Ashton Kutcher	Avril Lavigne	Bernie Mac
Beyoncé	Bow Wow	Britney Spears
Carrie Underwood	Chris Brown	Chris Daughtry
Christina Aguilera	Christopher Paul Curtis	Ciara
Clay Aiken	Condoleezza Rice	Daniel Radcliffe
David Ortiz	Derek Jeter	Eminem
Eve	Fergie (Stacy Ferguson)	50 Cent
Gwen Stefani	Ice Cube	Jamie Foxx
Ja Rule	Jay-Z	Jennifer Lopez
Jessica Simpson	J. K. Rowling	Johnny Depp
JoJo	Justin Berfield	Justin Timberlake
Kate Hudson	Keith Urban	Kelly Clarkson
Kenny Chesney	Lance Armstrong	Lindsay Lohan
Mariah Carey	Mario	**Mary J. Blige**
Mary-Kate and Ashley Olsen	Michael Jackson	Miguel Tejada
Missy Elliott	Nancy Pelosi	Nelly
Orlando Bloom	P. Diddy	Paris Hilton
Peyton Manning	Queen Latifah	Ron Howard
Rudy Giuliani	Sally Field	Selena
Shakira	Shirley Temple	Tim McGraw
Usher	Zac Efron	

Library of Congress Cataloging-in-Publication Data
Torres, Jennifer.
    Mary J. Blige / by Jennifer Torres.
        p. cm. — (Blue banner biographies)
    Includes bibliographical references and index.
    ISBN 978-1-58415-612-3 (library bound)
    1. Blige, Mary J.—Juvenile literature. 2. Rap musicians—United States—Biography—Juvenile literature. I. Title.
ML3930.B585T67 2007
782.421643092—dc22
[B]   2007000663

ABOUT THE AUTHOR: Jennifer Torres is a freelance writer and newspaper columnist based in Central Florida. Her articles have appeared in newspapers, parenting journals, and women's magazines across the United States and Canada. When she's not writing she enjoys spending time at the beach with her husband, John, and their five children, Timothy, Emily, Isabelle, Daniel, and Jacqueline.

PHOTO CREDITS: Cover—Frank Micelotta/Getty Images; pp. 4, 7—Tim Mosenfelder/Getty Images; p. 12—Getty Images; p. 14—Bryan Bedder/Getty Images; p. 18—Andrew D. Bernstein/ NBAE/Getty Images; p. 20—Scott Gries/ImageDirect; p. 23—Dave Hogan/Getty Images; p. 25—Charley Gallay/Getty Images; p. 27—Getty Images.

Although Mary had tough times as a child, she managed to use her talent, wits, and determination to escape the drugs and desperation that dominated her scary neighborhood.

Tough Times

*I*t was a day just like any other. As Mary Jane Blige rubbed the sleep from her eyes, she took a deep breath. Another day without sunshine.

Mary forced herself out of bed and glanced out the window. The sky was gray and overcast. Dark clouds hung over the Schlobam housing projects where Mary lived. Housing projects are apartment homes owned by the government, which rents them to people who don't have a lot of money. While many projects can offer a nice environment, the one Mary lived in was a scary place. People nicknamed it "Slow Bomb" because a lot of bad things happened there, like fights, burglaries, and gang activity.

As Mary looked out over the projects, she felt sad. Her father had left her family and her life long ago. She didn't know why he'd decided to go away, but she did know it left her mother very bitter and unhappy. That made Mary even sadder.

Life had gotten even more difficult over the previous year. Mary was spending time with friends who didn't really care about her. They told her it was cool to drink and do drugs. Because Mary didn't have a lot of self-esteem, she did what they said.

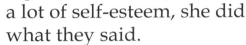

Life had gotten even more difficult over the previous year. Mary was spending time with friends who didn't really care about her.

The decision to live an unhealthy life didn't just mean that Mary felt angry, sad, and unhappy; it also meant that she couldn't concentrate on her schoolwork. At the age of 16, Mary had decided to quit school. Now at 17, she had all day to do nothing.

As she thought about her bad choices, tears fell down her face. They felt hot, and she quickly wiped them away. She was tough. She didn't cry. What would her friends think?

But she knew she didn't have real friends.

Since she wasn't in school, Mary spent her time wandering around the projects with other people who had dropped out. She also made a little money by cutting the hair of people in her building, including several of her aunts who lived nearby. She didn't like them very much. They were always telling her she wouldn't amount to anything. She was beginning to think they were right.

Mary realized she had made a mistake when she dropped out of high school. "If I had the sense that I have now back then, I would be in college by now," she told Jet *magazine. "I would have had a bachelor's degree and all of that by now. Education is important no matter what field you want to go into." She added, "Take your education seriously. . . . Things are not looking like they are getting easier. It looks like it's going to be even harder to find a job without at least a high school education."*

This day, though, she wasn't cutting hair. She had different plans. Mary and a few of her friends were heading to White Plains, New York, to visit the shopping mall. White Plains was a ritzy place with fancy stores and beautiful houses. She often imagined what life must be like for the teenagers who grew up in such grand-looking homes. People with money must not have any problems, she thought. Their lives must be so happy and easy. She wondered why her life was so hard.

There was one thing that made her happy, though, and that was singing. As a young girl she often sang in church. . . .

There was one thing that made her happy, though, and that was singing. As a young girl she often sang in church and everyone there would tell her how beautiful her voice was. But at home, no one encouraged her — not her aunts, not her cousins, no one. They all laughed and made fun of her. Even her mom.

Later in life, Mary would think back as to why that was. Her mother was a big fan of music and had wanted a career as a singer but never went for it. This probably made her a little jealous of Mary's success. "This is the career she wanted and she didn't have the courage to pursue it," Mary said in an interview with a London newspaper.

When Mary was a young girl, her mother's attitude was confusing, and it caused Mary and her mother to slowly grow apart.

On this day, however, Mary wasn't listening to the negative people all around her. She was going to the mall in White Plains for one reason, and it wasn't to buy clothes or shoes or records. She was taking some of the money she'd earned cutting hair to a place in the mall where she could sing a song and have it recorded. It was kind of a low-tech music studio for the masses. Anyone could walk in, pay a little money, and sing a song of their choice to prerecorded music. It was like karaoke. The song was recorded on a tape, and that's what you got to take home.

It's just for fun, thought Mary. No big deal at all.

How wrong she would be.

> *Mary was taking some of the money she'd earned cutting hair to a place in the mall where she could sing a song and have it recorded.*

A Hard Road

Mary Jane Blige was born on January 11, 1971, in the Bronx, New York, to Thomas and Cora Blige. The Bronx is one of New York City's five boroughs and home to the New York Yankees. However, Mary and her family did not attend any baseball games.

When she reached the age of four, her father announced he was leaving. Devastated and afraid of being a single mother, Cora took Mary and her older sister, LaTonya, with her to Savannah, Georgia, where they could be near family — including Mary's grandmother.

"When he left, I was four. But he would come back and forth. You know, like I saw him again when I was around nine. And then I never saw him again after that. And he was like everything to me," Blige said. "He was the type of man that I wanted. He was handsome. He was a musician. He was just everything that I loved him so much."

Perhaps Mary wanted him to be something he wasn't, and she saw what she wanted to see. During a 2006 appearance on *The Oprah Winfrey Show*, she admitted to remembering more of what life with him was like. She said: "He was hard on us and he made us spell words, like whatever month we were in, he made us spell it. And if we couldn't spell that word, that month that we were in, he made us go in the corner and with one leg stand there for like hours if we couldn't spell it. So, I mean, I don't know how—how to take that, as abuse or what."

Oprah's answer was instant. "It is. That is called abuse."

Unlike the Bronx, Savannah was full of wide-open spaces and lots of green grass. But what started as a new beginning became a nightmare. At the age of five, a relative began abusing her. It was a horrible memory she lived with for years.

She said, "I began to just pray and ask God to show me, who am I? I need to know who I am. So once He showed me, it hurt. It hurt to find out that I was all these things that I was. The key was

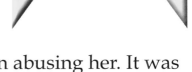

Perhaps Mary wanted him to be something he wasn't, and she saw what she wanted to see.

Over the years, Mary J. Blige and television personality Oprah Winfrey have become very close. Mary J. has appeared on Oprah's talk show several times, where she has revealed painful childhood memories. The two often appear together at charity, sporting, and other events. In 2007, Blige attended the opening of Oprah Winfrey's Leadership Academy for Girls in South Africa.

forgiveness, forgiving myself for, you know, being so hard on myself, because it wasn't my fault."

Within a couple years of arriving in Georgia, Mary's mother decided they should moved back to New York. Times were tough. Without a lot of money, their options were limited, so they moved into the Schlobam housing projects in Yonkers, an old mill town on the Hudson River in New York.

Eventually her mother remarried and had two more children, Jonquell and Bruce. They all barely fit in the small apartment, but Mary would often escape by going to church. She loved church, a place where they encouraged her to do something she loved — sing.

And sing she did. Every chance she got. At the age of seven she began singing solos in the choir. Everyone seemed to enjoy hearing her — except, of course, for those closest to her.

They all barely fit in the small apartment, but Mary would often escape by going to church.

"I knew in my heart, from when I was seven years old, that something big was going to happen to me through singing, but people were always flushing my dreams down the toilet," Blige said.

Mary loved to spend hours listening to her mother's favorite records. Her collection included Otis Redding, Gladys Knight, Al Green, and Donny Hathaway.

As she grew, the sounds of her neighborhood also began to sink in. The walls were thin in the projects, and the pulsing sound of hip-hop would come right in as her neighbors hosted party after party.

As Mary J. took in the sounds of hip-hop, soul, and her neighborhood, her dreams of becoming a singer grew. Despite the negativity of people around her, she became extremely successful. By 2007, she had sold over 34 million records worldwide.

She wanted to be a singer so badly, but by the time she reached the age of 16, Mary realized that most of the people around her were not going to cheer her on. During an interview later in life, she said, "[I realized] that no one [was] where I really needed them, to cheer me on, to say, 'Mary, you can sing.' "

But someone very important was about to give her more support than she ever dreamed possible.

Big Break

A knock at the door disrupted her thoughts. It was Mary's friends, and they were ready to go to the mall.

Once there, the girls found the recording studio. Mary paid a fee to the lady at the front desk and was taken to a small room with a microphone in the center. In front of her was a copy of lyrics to Anita Baker's song "Caught Up in the Rapture."

The music took over and she forgot she was in the mall, in a small little room. Suddenly she was on stage, and she belted out the song. As she left, Mary was handed a small cassette tape of her work.

As Mary made her way back home that night, little did she know that what she held in her hand would open the door to whole new world.

Mary loved the tape and played it often. Surprisingly, her stepfather, James Dillard, loved it too. One day he asked if he could borrow it. He knew a few people who worked in the music industry.

None of them was famous, but he figured they might be able to get the tape to someone who was.

He passed the tape on, and that person sent it on to someone else, and it traveled from person to person, until one day it landed in the hands of Andre Harrell. Harrell was the chief executive officer of Uptown Records — in a position to make Mary a star. He liked what he heard.

One day, the phone rang in Mary's small apartment. It was a phone call that would change her life.

One day, the phone rang in Mary's small apartment. It was a phone call that would change her life. It was Andrew Harrell, and he wanted to see Mary in person. All this time, no one had paid attention to her music; now someone who knew music was paying attention to her.

Things moved quickly from there. When Mary met with Harrell, she was nervous but also confident. She was sitting in a big office of a big music industry producer — and he liked her — she could tell. When she sang for him, he just stared in amazement.

Not long after that, Harrell offered Mary a contract. It didn't take more than a moment for Mary to sign it. She didn't even really read it, but she knew it meant a chance to sing for real, and she wasn't about to pass it up.

"I didn't have a class in accounting," Mary said. "I didn't read the contract that I signed. I just wanted my mother out of the ghetto, so I signed it, you know."

By signing, she became Uptown's first female artist — and its youngest.

Mary had to begin at the beginning, and that meant serving as a backup singer to acts that were already established. In 1990, she performed in a live show as a backup singer for Jeff Redd. The show was at the Apollo, a famous stage in Harlem, New York. It was exciting, but she didn't get a lot of attention.

Mary had to begin at the beginning, and that meant serving as a backup singer to acts that were already established.

Later that year she was given the chance to sing the hook, or the line that is repeated over and over, almost like the chorus, in the song "I'll Do 4 U." The song was by rapper Father MC, another artist signed by Uptown. Mary even got to appear in the video, but once again, only as a backup singer.

At about the same time, Sean "Puffy" Combs, known today as P. Diddy or just Diddy, was an

Mary J. and producer Sean "Diddy" Combs have been working together since around 1990. They would become friends, boost each other's careers, go their separate ways, and become friends again.

up-and-coming young producer at Uptown Records. He was looking for talent. He wanted to work with people he knew had star potential. If he found the right people, not only could he make their career pop, but they could make his skyrocket.

When he heard a tape of Mary J., he was impressed. He saw star potential.

Together they would make history.

CHAPTER 4

What's the 411?

Mary had the sound, but she needed style. Puffy had plenty of style to go around. He was flashy, but he worked hard and he knew how to take something good and make it great. That's what he wanted to do with Mary.

As for Mary, she loved the attention. She was ready to come out from the background and take her place front and center.

The people she worked with, including Puffy, had become family. She trusted him. He dressed her in a hip street style and gave her music to sing that had a tough edge. They put together an album, called *What's the 411?* It was a hit.

Suddenly Mary was Mary J., and she had her first top ten single, "Real Love." However, real love was not something Mary had. Even though the album sold more than two million copies worldwide, Mary still didn't feel that different from the girl who lived in the projects. "Be careful what you ask for, because real love is not people yes-maam-ing you to death," Blige said. "Real love is painful, in a good way, because real love is finding out who you are."

Mary did not yet know who she was.

However, the world seemed to. They dubbed her "The Queen of Hip-Hop Soul."

When she released her first album, Mary still didn't know who she was. It would take years of soul-searching before she'd feel confident in herself.

Later in an interview, Puffy would reflect on his time with Mary in an interview. "Mary's music has been a reflection of her life. A lot of women all over the world can relate to it: the ups and downs, the struggles, and the triumphs that women go through. And Mary has been open and honest more than most people would be."

Puffy also worked with Mary on her follow-up album, which was called *My Life*. It went multi-platinum, meaning it sold millions of copies. She won a Grammy Award for Best Rap Performance by a Duo or Group.

In a review of the album, Stanton Swihart of *All Music Guide* said, "Perhaps the single finest moment in Sean 'Puffy' Combs' musical career has been the production on this, Mary J. Blige's second proper album."

> "Mary's music has been a reflection of her life. A lot of women all over the world can relate to it. . . ."

Even with all the successes, Mary's life began to spiral. Moving out of the projects had not healed the hurt she had inside. She wasn't surrounded by the same people, but strangely, they were the same. Drugs, drinking, and excess were everywhere. People who said they were her friends convinced her to party and have fun.

She wasn't taking care of herself. She felt tired. Bad relationships and bad personal choices wreaked havoc on her. Songs like the one titled "I'm Going Down" should have served as a warning to her friends.

Mary also began to worry about everything and everyone around her. She stopped trusting people, including Puffy.

Mary also began to worry about everything and everyone around her. She stopped trusting people, including Puffy. As a producer, Puffy worked with other singers too. Mary began to get jealous of this, especially when she noticed that he began to groom another young female singer just like her.

"He had signed a female artist that they were giving my image to, my sound to, and he was co-managing me. And I said, 'Well, I can't—this is too much.' Like I'm looking in a magazine thinking I'm looking at me, and I'm looking at her. So this was like, huh-uh, you know, I'm going to go over here," Blige said. "I love you. I'm going to do this, but I can't do this because it's going to suck all the life out of me. So I went and I did 'Share My World,' which debuted at number one. Mary did it by herself."

Mary J. performs with British pop star Elton John at Madison Square Garden in New York. Throughout her career, she has collaborated with many great musicians. Her 1999 album Mary *featured songs she performed with Elton John, Eric Clapton, Lauryn Hill, and Aretha Franklin.*

The album was a change for Mary. Not only had she let go of some old friends, she let go of some bad habits.

She wanted to be happy. She had the money, she had the fame—now she wanted peace. She didn't want to hurt anymore. She didn't want the drama.

No More Drama

Her next album, simply titled *Mary*, came out in 1999. It was a change from everything that came before. The hard edge had softened and taken on some real soul. And this time, Mary had the help of a few new friends, among them Elton John, Stevie Wonder, Lauryn Hill, and even one of her mother's favorite singers, Aretha Franklin.

Her most personal album to date came in 2001 with the release of *No More Drama*. This time, Mary wrote songs from the heart—songs that talked about her desire for peace, happiness, and real love. It was very different from *What's the 411?* This album wasn't about flash. It was about substance.

In 2003, Mary reunited with an old friend, P. Diddy, for *Love and Life*. "First time I heard Mary J. Blige sing, her voice was so rough, it was so pure, it was so from the heart. I knew that—I knew that she would be a giant. Musically, she had such an impact on me, and I think I had such an impact on her. It was just inevitable that we'd come back together," P. Diddy said. "Whenever I think of Mary, I think about her smiling, because I know the whole history of Mary. I know how long it took her to get to that point to smile."

Mary had a lot to smile about then. The year 2003 was also when she married the love of her life, Kendu Isaacs. "I believe in love. I believe good relationships do exist, but you've got to have a love affair with yourself first and really know yourself from the inside out before you can have a good relationship with a

When Mary J. married Kendu Isaacs, her life had turned around — again. She had stopped drinking and taking drugs, and, she says, she finally felt love. In March 2006, she told Rolling Stone, *"For the first time in my life, I'm proud of myself."*

man or anyone else," she said in an interview. She also became stepmom to his two children.

Mary had stopped drinking, stopped taking drugs, and started living her life the way she always knew she could. She felt she had the love of not only Isaacs but also of God. "I knew that love was going to come, and it didn't have to come from a man. It came from 'The Man.' . . . God gave me that self love, and from that I was able to draw even more love."

Her journey wasn't easy, but Mary wouldn't have it any other way. Because then she just wouldn't be the Mary she is today.

Two more Grammy Awards followed in 2002 and 2003. In December 2005, she joined forces again with Diddy to produce the powerful *Breakthrough.* The album debuted at number one on the Billboard chart, selling 727,000 copies in its first week. It gained her eight Grammy nominations and three wins: Best Female R&B Vocal Performance and Best R&B Song for "Be Without You," and Best R&B Album.

In 2006, she released *Reflections: A Retrospective.* It would include past hits plus four new songs.

In June 2007, Mary was honored with the ASCAP Voice of Music Award, which is given to artists "whose music illuminates people's lives through song." "To many, Mary J. Blige is not only the 'Queen of Hip-Hop Soul,' but also a guiding light," said Marilyn Bergman, ASCAP President and Chairman. "Through all of her struggles, she was determined to find and maintain her own musical voice. . . . The ASCAP Voice of Music Award is an honor that she richly deserves."

Her journey wasn't easy, but Mary wouldn't have it any other way. Because then she just wouldn't be the Mary she is today. And she likes her — a lot.

"From self-hate and self-pity to self-knowledge," Blige said. "From being my own worst enemy and

Mary J. records a cover of the Eric Clapton song "Tears in Heaven." The proceeds from the record would go to help children who were affected by the Asian tsunami of 2004.

blaming everyone else for the things that have happened to me, to learning that I have to take responsibility for myself. It's a breakthrough from ignorance."

Mary serves as an inspiration for many young girls who come from tough beginnings. She likes to be seen as an example of how far you can come with determination, even when others put you down.

She also speaks out about not using drugs, making public service announcements and working with anti-drug education groups. She received the *Rolling Stone* Do Something Award for her charity work, which includes raising money for AIDS education and research. She also raised money for the victims of Hurricane Katrina, which struck the Gulf Coast states in 2005.

Mary always wanted to be a hero for other girls going through hard times. No one was there to encourage her when she was young, but plenty of people told her she should give up. Despite that, Mary kept hope alive. She believed she was meant to sing, even when others pushed her down.

For Mary, heroes were hard to come by. When she was a little girl, the only heroes she knew were the ones on television. "It was *Super Friends* that did it for me," Blige said. "I grew up watching *Super Friends,* and looking back on it now, I like the fact that at the end of every show they'd always deliver some kind of message. You know, it was usually about telling kids to help others or something like that. I listened to those messages. I still live by them today."

1971   Mary Jane Blige is born on January 11 in the Bronx, New York.

1975   Mary's father leaves the family. Mary, her mother, and her sister move to Savannah, Georgia. A few years later, they return to New York.

1988   At the age of 17, Mary records "Caught Up in the Rapture" at the mall. The tape is later passed on to Uptown Records.

1989   Mary signs a recording contract with Uptown Records

1992   Mary's first album, *What's the 411?*, is released and sells more than two million copies worldwide.

1994   Her follow-up album, *My Life*, goes multi-platinum and generates several hit singles.

1995   Mary wins a Grammy Award for Best Rap Performance by a Duo or Group.

2000   She receives the *Rolling Stone* Do Something Award for her charity work for AIDS fund-raising and anti-drug public service announcements.

2002   She wins a Grammy Award for Best Female R&B Vocal Performance for "He Think I Don't Know."

2003   She marries Kendu Isaacs. She re-teams with P. Diddy for *Love and Life*. She wins a Grammy Award for Best Pop Collaboration with Vocals for "Whenever I Say Your Name," with Sting.

2005   P. Diddy produces her album *The Breakthrough*, which is released in December.

2006   She releases *Reflections: A Retrospective*, and *Mary J. Blige and Friends.*

2007   She wins a Grammy and a Soul Train Music Award for best female album for *The Breakthrough*, and two more Grammys for "Be Without You." She is named Best Female Artist by the NAACP. She is honored with the ASCAP Voice of Music Award. Throughout her career, she has sold over 34 million records worldwide.

DISCOGRAPHY

1992 *What's the 411?*
1994 *My Life*
1997 *Share My World*
1999 *Mary*
2001 *No More Drama*
2003 *Love and Life*
2005 *The Breakthrough*
2006 *Reflections: A Retrospective*
     Mary J. Blige & Friends

FURTHER READING

For Young Readers
Brown, Terrell. *Mary J. Blige.* Broomall, Pennsylvania: Mason Crest Publishers, 2006.
Torres, John. *P. Diddy.* Hockessin, Delaware: Mitchell Lane Publishers, 2005.

Works Consulted
"ASCAP to Honor Mary J. Blige at 20th Anniversary Rhythm and Soul Music Awards Celebration," ASCAP Press Release, May 15, 2007. http://www.ascap.com/press/2007/051507_rsawards.html
Edwards, Gavin. *Rolling Stone: The Continuing Drama of Mary J. Blige,* March 10, 2006, http://www.rollingstone.com/news/story/9447919/the_continuing_drama_of_mary_j_blige
Husband, Stuart. *The Taming of a Diva* (London: Mail on Sunday), February 14, 2006.

"Mary J. Blige Tells Why Dropping Out of High School Was a Big Mistake." *Jet*, November 29, 1999. http://findarticles.com/p/articles/mi_m1355/is_26_96/ai_58342847

"Mary J. Blige Reveals Almost All," *The Guardian*, December 19, 2005, http://playahata.com/hatablog/?p=1148

Morgan, Joan. "What You Never Knew About Mary—Mary J. Blige—Interview" *Essence*, November 2001.

The Oprah Winfrey Show, February 1, 2006.

The Oprah Winfrey Show, December 25, 2003.

Riemenschneider, Chris. "Call her SUPERDIVA; In ink or in the flesh, Mary J. Blige does it all," *The Austin American-Statesman*, 2000.

Schumacher-Rasmussen, Eric. "Mary J. Blige Honored for Charity Work," *VH-1 News*, November 21, 2000, http://www.vh1.com/artists/news/1274492/20001120/blige_mary_j.jhtml

On the Internet

The Official Site of Mary J. Blige
    www.mjblige.com

AOL Music. Mary J. Blige Biography
    http://music.aol.com/artist/mary-j-blige/57322/biography

The Oprah Winfrey Show; "Aretha Franklin and Mary J. Blige," September 24, 2003, http://www.oprah.com/tows/pastshows/200309/tows_past_20030924.jhtml

"Oprah's Cut with Mary J. Blige," *O, The Oprah Magazine*, May 2006, http://www.oprah.com/omagazine/200605/omag_200605_ocut.jhtml

Universal Urban: Mary J. Blige
    http://universalurban.com/maryjblige/

INDEX